IN THE
PERMANENT
COLLECTION

Poems by STEFANIF WORTMAN

University of North Texas Press, Denton, Texas

10 9 8 7 6 5 4 3 2 1

Permissions:
University of North Texas Press
1155 Union Circle #311336
Denton, TX 76203-5017

The paper used in this book meets the minimum requirements of the American National Standard for Permanence of Paper for Printed Library Materials, z39.48.1984. Binding materials have been chosen for durability.

Library of Congress Cataloging-in-Publication Data

Wortman, Stefanie, author.
In the permanent collection : poems / by Stefanie Wortman.
    pages cm—(Vassar Miller prize in poetry series ; no. 21)
Includes bibliographical references.
Vassar Miller Prize in Poetry, 2013.
ISBN 978-1-57441-554-4 (pbk. : alk. paper)—ISBN 978-1-57441-564-3 (ebook)
I. Title. II. Series: Vassar Miller prize in poetry series ; no. 21.
PS3623.O782I5 2014
811'.6—dc23

2013047884

In the Permanent Collection is Number 21 in the Vassar Miller Prize in Poetry Series

The electronic edition of this book was made possible by the support of the Vick Family Foundation.

Cover Illustration *Laocoon* is by Liane Lang. Used by permission.

for my mother, Becky
and my brother, Jason

CONTENTS

III

IV

ACKNOWLEDGMENTS

Grateful acknowledgment is made to the editors of the following journals, in which these poems previously appeared:

Alehouse: "Star Chart" and "Sleeping Song"

Antioch Review: "Permanent Collection"

Boston Review: "Blind King," "Likeness," "Vaudeville," and "You're in the Picture"

Cavalier Literary Couture: "To a Friend, on Living Alone"

Chariton Review: "Spiritual Exercises," "Strip Mall," "Weed Guide," and "The Zombie"

Cimarron Review: "Surrender"

Court Green: "A Story about Show Business"

Gargoyle: "Careless Simile"

Kenyon Review Online: "Lucky"

Memorious: "Long Occupation"

Muzzle: "Spring"

New Orleans Review: "The Transparent Fabulist"

Pleiades: "Everyone Was Dead and I Went On, Drunk"

Sixth Finch: "Low Definition"

Smartish Pace: "Mortuary Art" and "Reform, Missouri"

Subtropics: "Family Plot"

Sugar House Review: "*The Gallow Ball* (1950)"

Tusculum Review: "Reasons for Living Happily"

Whiskey Island: "Compact Mirror"

Yale Review: "Twelve Bar Blues"

Zócalo Public Square: "Sibling Gothic"

I am also grateful to the University of Missouri Department of English and the Kimmel Harding Nelson Center in Nebraska City, Nebraska, for support during the writing of this book. Thank you to my teachers and mentors: Lynne McMahon, Scott Cairns, Robert Pinsky, Rosanna Warren, Aliki Barnstone, and Alex Socarides. Thanks to Gabe Fried for unwavering belief in this book through its various stages and to Sarah Barber, Jessica Garratt, Katy Didden, Marc McKee, and Camellia Cosgray for generous reading and strict deadlines. Thanks to Rob Foreman for everything, including Moriah Foreman.

REFORM, MISSOURI

As a centipede twitches into the dark
of the electric burner, the winds that temper
weather whip over ice, give their hearts
to the winds of the abyss. When we were
tourists at Alcatraz, under the gun gallery,
we shivered at the clock that marked no incident
but sorrow. Beyond our own valley
of correction—adult intake, resident
juvenile detention—the nuclear plant's flood
lights warm the road to Reform. An eye
just blackened, its enraged white like blood
diluted to pink on the butcher's twine,
makes a smear of ink in a column of losses.
Watercolor poppies dot a field of crosses.

BLIND KING

Meaning installer of shades,
he who lets us play day
for night in the houses where

we are so unhappy. Contrary
to first appearance, this title
block-lettered on the van

stopped in traffic carries
no allusion to heedless power,
internecine battle, neither Lear

nor Gloucester who hails him:
The King is coming. The gentle-
man still sees. *Before I got my eye*

put out, writes Dickinson, pitying
the poor animals who look
and think it a pleasure. Then sight

is cheapest to those who never
see, or see with trouble? A patch
forces the lazy eye awake

while its legitimate brother
gives up and goes dark. In sunken
rooms, on scratchy rugs, maybe

we've never known happiness.
The servants are forced to watch
as their master digs his fingers

into the old man's sockets.
The least obedient among them
goes to *fetch some flax*

and whites of eggs to apply
to his bleeding face, finding
balm stronger, more coagulant,

than the noble son-in-law's
milky gentleness. A territory
cracked into jagged halves,

land that was so unhappy,
where we burned the faces
of men out of all the tapestries.

NEW ORLEANS

The highway overpass
Parts subtropic sea
In Mosaic fashion.
Video help my unbelief.

Revision of covenant:
Avoid saying *fault.*
Scratch out *feet to stand.*
For *seed* read *salt.*

No thumb for the dam,
A baby's in the breach,
One half for the pride of man,
The other for the king.

Who walks on water
Doesn't risk disease.
Forgive the daintiness.
Forgive the relief.

LOW DEFINITION

A goalie's throat bisected by a skate.
A pit bull accidentally shot in a drug raid.
Prince Ginger whom his comrades in war name
Bullet Catcher. A computer model of the blade
cutting through neck muscles. Cartilage
extracted by forceps, a piece of bone-sponge.
Blood slick on the ice. A police dredge
hauled through the riverside reed fringe.
These things I saw on TV. And next:
behind the urban prison's display glass,
a guard with a moustache directs
a man to remove his navy work pants,
his briefs. Does his face betray humiliation?
The jail, too, was designed for observation.

EVERYONE WAS DEAD AND I WENT ON, DRUNK

after Pierre Jean Jouve, "Ville atroce"

Savage city, capital of days. Oh sad
city, given up to the villainous cops.

I came to the avenues of fire
in glinting July with its million movable
joints, its parti-colored garments flying
from the roofs of the embassies.

Celebrated city, I saw your white stone
corpse, sprawling and multi-storied,
the Smithsonian reclined beneath the swag
of lavender sky, the accumulated offices

stretched out beyond the dry lawn.
Unmeasured ocean of peace and war, piling
up glories. Even there, I was surprised
into laughter before the blinding obelisk.

THE GENERAL

At the end of a dun decade,
just as the train pulled away
from the Pentagon stop, I saw
a man in dust-and-gravel
camouflage, pants tucked into tan
boots laced high over his ankles,
and in my mind I called him
The General because he looked
middle-aged and serious, dimple-
chinned, press-conference ready.

He stopped among commuters,
but he was for the desert, the one
landscape that we, the subconscious
ones, hope will blow away, as I
had hoped of my head-in-the-sand
week. Each night I was pursued
through dreams by the father
of a student who took an overdose.
He asked why I didn't notice
anything, and I was afraid.

Not that I felt safer when I saw
The General. I didn't want him
on that train, need him on that train,
but I liked his expressionless
face and straight back. I wondered
about the hard chest beneath
his tan jacket. I think I fell in
love with The General. I wanted
to shut his mouth with mine to keep
all the evil orders from spilling out.

WEED GUIDE

Soapweed yucca
in the back yard,
waxy seeds stacked
in pods I pick
apart. Jokers
used to call hemp
neckweed after
the hanging rope.
Even the site of
an oil spill will
flush with fireweed,
and starry chicory,
fringed periwinkle
flowers that turn
white in an hour
after being picked,
some call coffeeweed,
and some blue sailors.

CARELESS SIMILE

After the ice storm, glitter covers
the asphalt roadways. When I hear
someone say it's "like a war zone
down to the south," I can't believe it

because death does not descend here
as a stern angel with bruised eyes,
strong-tendoned wings that pass over
audible screams. He comes to eat

us slowly from inside, crunches
our trucks together in the deep
night, with no one awake to hear.
I read that after one of the West

Side Boys offered a choice of hands
to a gasping woman, he brought
the machete down across both
wrists. And while a photographer

sharpened his focus on the ends
of her abbreviated arms,
the refugee children took turns
trying her plastic prostheses

then abandoned them to the ground.
If this landscape is torn apart,
the limbs of the trees severed
and thrown down, it's the weather

that determines to engage us
in guerilla war, and our tenuous
quiet made of clichés hardens
in the glaring indivisible ice.

VAUDEVILLE

Seeing him, smart
in his suit tailored to where the surgeon's
cut meets the wooden

crutch, you wouldn't
imagine Clayton Bates crying backstage
at the Moulin Rouge

over the moves
that hurt so much, like the signature Jet Plane.
His gymnastic hops

on peg leg across
the Ed Sullivan stage do resemble flight
compared with this

homeless veteran
dragging his wheelchair with the heel
of one shoe. Maybe

once the man would
have worn a bruise-colored coat, red-brown
and brown-purple shot

with gold, and cranked
a hurdy-gurdy, the cylinder's surging drone
marking him to his place

in the taxonomy of beggars—
not the lowest station, one affording a modest
collar and small dog.

But he has no strings,
no steps, only the fighter pilots and spies
in his madcap rant.

STRIP MALL

Car windshield broken, taxes undone, and hungry?
Here are your needs resolved. Laundromat, jewelry store,
copy shop, bar: uniform siding and signage betraying
the likeness of demand, balanced on the quarter point
of interest that stabilizes securities and prevents a real
estate bubble. The ice cream parlor shunting customers
into the dentist's chair, the sex shop providing penitents
to the church, brought, by an invisible hand, together
on these yards of asphalt. No developer's foresight
in such felicitous connections, such perfect commerce
of carpet sales and vacuum repair, rows of glassed shops
clinging to minor highways and busy side streets,
keeping things stop-and-go long into the evening.

LONG OCCUPATION

I was naïve of foreign affairs in the Four
Seasons bar when a Swiss knife maker
assured me of the coming war. I ignored,

the night of invasion, the accidental celebration
of a bottle of wine opened in spite of everything.
Four years later my radio wakes to a string

of explosions unreadable as fever or a blush
to lips pressed to the brow, indistinguishable
as our ones from one hundreds to the discerning

fingers of the blind. Sleep heavy as a child's
has impressed the red shape of my right hand
on my chest. In my university town, steel I-beams

rise out of the perfected pit of a new foundation,
a new addition to Physics. From down the street,
the welder's torch looks like a fallen star.

TWELVE BAR BLUES

A new mom's prone to get depressed
A new mom's prone to get depressed
Not just because she may not get undressed
Again in the mind of the checkout boy
    In the mind of the checkout boy
Or she's not used to the baby's noise
At least wanting something lets you
    Wanting something lets you
Know which way is up God bless you
If you know what's at the back of it
If you know what's at the back of it
If you can tell the blues from love and lack of it

RECOVERY COFFEE

On Sunday morning, smokers gathered
outside the coffee shop offer weekend
temptations for discussion. The twelve-
steppers resisted with varied degrees
of success. One asks, "Have you told
your problems how big your God is?"
Less reflective sinners have given
in wholly, returned with irritated faces.
Inside, one woman wants to recount
a visit from her mother-in-law while another
tries to explain the hard-living girlfriends
of her boyfriend's bandmates. A man
in a T-shirt that reads "Get your ass
to church" orders a cup of tea then adds
a splash of coffee and some cream.
We're all recovering from something.
I'm getting over (what else?) a bad love
that makes everything seem like direct
revelation—songs, especially, but also
bits of conversation. I overheard, "If you
don't want a haircut, stay out of the
barber shop," which, of course, made me
feel shorn. Yesterday the water
was tea-brown in the little subdivision
lake. The line of the shore, the shape
of a kiss, the lips, a leaf, the metaphor
lost now. The specials board offers
Minestrone and a soup called Happiness
(really!) made with yellow squash, lemon,
and basmati rice. Through the window
I watch a cardinal in the spare sidewalk tree,

orange beak chattering in her dark face.
Behind her, a moving van that has been
parked in the same spot for days gathers
tickets in pink envelopes. Some teenagers
have a dog who holds so fiercely to his
rope toy that he can be lifted off the ground,
his body hanging, tensed, his eyes bulging
but matter-of-fact. As I swing open the door
to leave, I almost hit a woman who ducks
her head like a shy girl. I want to tell her
to buck up, stop looking apologetic, but I know
what it's like. I'm sorry for my rush to get out,
for how clumsy everything is. I know the older
we get, the longer it takes to recover.

SIBLING GOTHIC

My tomatoes don't grow, or they grow
too big, black starbursts spreading
over the stem ends. With yellow-
stained hands, I brush off the ants
that patrol the edge of an oozing split.

As we spread out straw mulch, my brother
warns me of the things he's found baled up
before: dead mice and snake heads cut
by the combine. He found the deer skull
too when we were kids. We knocked

the dirt off and stuck it on a post
along our favorite path to a trio of rocks,
a tiny waterfall. We drank fistfuls
scooped up between the skating bugs,
swished the water through our teeth.

Whatever may have died upstream
transfused us equally. The bird carcass
he turns up now is hollow needles
tucked in vellum, nitrogen and phosphate
for the soil, bonemeal and bloodmeal.

THE TRANSPARENT FABULIST

Part air the hollow
boned bird. Eats
and eats until she
says she can't breathe.
That the spoon is
not itself but emptiness.
Flits out and comes
back lighter. Through
a skin the glass
frog's working organs.

THERE'S SOMETHING QUIETER
THAN SLEEP

I didn't call the Hospice,
only took my pew:
dark-suited with a white corsage,
a paper bent in two.

A last gift still counts on my wrist
the hours minutes make.
When the teeth shear off the gears,
I'll drop it in the lake.

It's not as if he didn't
mostly try to do things right.
I tender tears a few at a time,
my losses amortized.

FAMILY PLOT

Wind-scoured in fallow land,
bone orchard sheltered
in the airplane's shadow,
its incorporated space: a safe

place to be dead. The car
upturned on Barry Road.
Barbara in the hospital, Becky
at the stove, stirring the hollowed

house full of pepper smell.
Through a veil of dust the rare
truck treads up, the morning
fox's muzzle frets a footprint,

the scent we leave there,
the headstone's lamb's
prayer, thaw and thistle
bristling at the cemetery border.

PERMANENT COLLECTION

In the gallery of casts, a copy of the broken
Laocoön, improperly restored, extends his right
arm up from the shoulder. I would have guessed
the same about how to position it, not only for drama
in reaching to the gods, but also because it lengthens
the taut diagonal of his strained torso and left thigh.
His young sons, too, stretch fingers to the sky.
His mouth falls open in a noble kind of agony.

Twice a day I pass a more modest bit of sculpture:
in the window of a law office, two birds cast
in metal, not in flight but focused on the ground,
looking for crumbs maybe, matte grey heads turned
away from one another. Image not of crisis but grim
forbearance, these birds seem made to withstand
and at the same time made for nothing at all,
and in this they make me think of my father,
to whose mouth there was nothing classical,
who squinted into his life as if it were hard
to look at. As far as I know, he had few ideas
about art, probably wouldn't have paid much
attention to the photo on the cover of his funeral
program, but among the brocade colors
of its still-life fruits and flowers, the open throat
of a French horn was trite and a little distasteful.

Really I came today to see some borrowed
Parisian lithographs. But then, as I'm heading
upstairs, another copy stops me, the drain cover
set into floor tiles a miniature of the old priest Laocoön's
head and torso. He's alone this time, arm posed
the way scholars now think is right, bent at the elbow,

fist pulled back behind his head. The art in this fixture
is as weird to me as those ghosts of masterpieces
crowded into a room painted bluer than sky could
ever be, where among the gods and soldiers,
just to the side of the little family bound together
by snakes, a woman from Herculaneum, her face set
in a nurse's bland concern, draws her wrap
like a hood over her scalloped head, pleating
the fabric with her bleached plaster hands.

TELL ME ABOUT THE FATES

The boat jumped, the line pulled taut
and the tip of a pinky finger, caught
in a loop, was severed and dropped

in the water. Years contract to minutes
and I imagine my father's lost digit
in the sediment, nibbled by minnows.

Better maybe if he had lost an arm,
held off, by excising a larger part,
that malignancy, heavy but afloat.

So easy to imagine a patterned future,
but expecting the pains to pay is futile.
At most you get a few jokes and sutures.

YOU'RE IN THE PICTURE

The characters are outside in the courtyard
where they perform enjoyment for the sun,

appearing as lively as people should—
but the people are inside, just eating,

sleeping, or taking showers. They display
murky reasoning, serve unclear purposes.

My old roommate is a person, but married
to a character. They have a child who might,

for all I know, be either. He likes trucks
and trains, watches his father drive, wonders

what it means to control this mover that acts
both like and unlike an animal. A memoirist

I met calls himself a character, both a necessity
and a danger in his line of work. He should know

that characters have bigger stories, but people
have more of them. For whom am I a character

and for whom am I real? As I ask this question,
there you are, making a very small story

at the window, where you look out to see a pickup
clip a dog's leg and the dog vanish between houses.

MORTUARY ART

Again my mother makes me promise
never to have her cremated, as if I could
forget how different she and I are in our
senseless fears. I am so scared of burial,
that airless allotment of space the body
doesn't need. But maybe she's right
that grief should have a place to focus it.
You watch three pounds of ash dissolve
in water and suddenly, he's everywhere,
the dead father, in the rivulet rain makes
on your windshield. Instead, allow
the stone's symbolism, the highway
memorial cross's ruthless precision,
even if implicating the faded grass
along the margin is almost, no is,
too much to bear. Who knows how
the dead feel about our solicitude.
Whether we fold them, gently, lovingly,
or not, into a coffin, into a box, they are
not folded, are not there, are not.

TO MY HEART

Heart, I think if I could run you
under the faucet you would clean up
your act and be dignified for a change,
instead of jumping to fix your lipstick
every time someone new showed up
at the party.
      You feel like a box
that gets stuffed with styrofoam.
You're certain to make a mess.
Does it sound too zen to say you
should just embrace emptiness?
Anyway, heart, with you around
these questions will always be
academic.
      I try to imagine you
on fire, but your constant thump
insists you are not flammable.
You're muscular and wet like a particular
kind of unpleasant handshake. Lucky
for us both there are worse things
in the world.
      In preschool, my test
was an outlined person to fill in.

I drew you in the middle and wrote
beep beep, which goes to show I've had
the wrong idea about you all along.

THE ZOMBIE

arrived in the mail along with a tin of tea leaves
and a gold fabric bag holding a handful of dice
for a game I don't recognize. One roll turns up
a nine of clubs, a suitless queen, and a blank.
Did the one who sent them think I was a cipher?
He asked "tell me something," meaning anything.
Now I take out these small gifts, and they seem
rich with meaning, but I can't make them speak
out of their kraft paper wrapping. I think I like
them more now that they don't matter much.
He and I can be both or neither: the black string
zombie doll with a satiny red heart and a chain
on his head or the bookmark sandalwood elephant.

CAVEBUNNY

Elsewhere in the defunct prison, we find traces
of personal beefs or gang battle, like a bug-eyed
cartoon with menacing caption—*I'm watching
you, Jerry*—but here, in the former visiting room,
waits a papier-mâché, stone age fantasy girl,
from an era of lawless clubbings, before lethal
injection or electrocution, before rope, before
anything but male, female, child, and fire
in a domestic scene. The man's face has
been stripped to reveal the chicken wire
an inmate molded then plastered over,
but the kid was spared for sentiment's sake,
and the woman looks perfect, as if carved
out of sugar, leaning forward on the log
where some convict posed her to arch
her back, round her ass, this proto-pinup,
out of time before silver silhouettes on mud-
flaps, before anything but the gravity of breasts.

TENNESSEE WILLIAMS

He heard Miss So-and-So was back in Rome
and had a new friend with an ass just like
a Macon pony's, so to avoid the psych
ward and the drink, he bought a ticket home.
He wanted to be in Key West, with its good
weather and cruising and the feeling you
are out on the cuff of the world—although his blue
devils muscled in there to show they could
survive the afternoons. While the skylight's
geometry traversed the table, he
dug through Crane for a title, found the scene
of a jumper pitched into a bay like eyes
rolling around him. Beneath the wave there came
a white sea turtle and nudged the boy away.

SURRENDER

After René Char, "L'Innofensif"

I cry when the sun goes to bed because he undresses you in front of me and because I can't get along with his nighttime rivals. He's gone down now, his fever has gone down, and there's no point in struggling with him, trying to pull up one last shoot from his warm bed. The obscurity he leaves behind dissolves you as stormwater thins silt beyond the landslide of a ruined bank. Hardness and softness in different sources have the same end. The song of your speech is exhausted. This thing in my hand isn't the linchpin of your wrist but a stick from the woodbox. We don't give a name to anything now except the shivers. It's night. The blind lights switch on in my face.

Really I have only cried one time. The falling sun slashed your neck. Your head rolled in the grave of the sky, and then I couldn't believe in the morning.

And the man of morning, which of these is his shadow?

TO A FRIEND, ON LIVING ALONE

Last night while I stood just inside, my hand
feeling the door rattle, as whoever was knocking,
probably wanting only to sell me cable service or candy,
banged again, and I wondered whether to click the lock,
alert the fist under its pounding that I was there,
scared, I thought of you. When we met again
on the steps to the building after getting into different
strangers' cars, the relief on your face was beautiful
beneath the streetlamp. As an art school friend said,
Honey, you can't have *clair-obscur* without a bright light.
And tomorrow, your eyes aqua like the pool
of a drained fountain, or a pale electrical-storm green,
you can have the cold moonlight of cucumbers
in phases on the cutting board, their taste of wet grass.

SPRING

The muscle pulsing in the back of a man's shoulder as his
    finger drums the tabletop
and the lipstick mark of a nipple through his white shirt are
    none of my business.

Back home, the ugly irises button up like Victorian ladies
    with Gibson hairdos,
magnolias put on their waxy blush, and mowers break wild
    onions in the ditch.

I wish I knew what your wife looks like so I could imagine
    her getting fat.
There. After all the awful thoughts I forced you to, we can
    start to call it even.

The first thing I reach for is never the thing I need. I dump
    the whole jewelry box
into my lap: acid green glass, sparks of marcasite, buffed knots
    of pearl.

A STORY ABOUT SHOW BUSINESS

The Devils take a boy out of his company
town. The linebacker takes a steak house
in Steeple City. The charcoal man takes
an insurance agent's daughter who puts on
a feathered follies hat. The throaty singer
takes a slugger on a streak. The all-time
all-star takes a model who can tell a joke.
The bombshell, stitched up in her nudity
dress, takes the flashbulbs' hard slaps.

STAR CHART

Like sweat, the sign of his mouth evaporates
on her neck. She's thinking of the planets spinning
through zones that regulate her luck in love
or finance. He blames these moods on her friends
and their young men, struggling all the time
to stay together or apart. He knows
how our paths look purposeful if considered
from a distance. Those teenaged couples
who name imaginary children wouldn't dream
of numbering the string of cars they'll drive
or minor surgeries endure. And his love—
anticipating fictions, she expects
the death of a parent, but not the death of a pet.

He's wrung disruptions large and small
through habit, and what survives clouds
like glass scraped by the river's sandy tongue.
A scattering of pills on the night stand
forms its own zodiac, and if he spins
into the house of Xanax, it isn't chance
but willful ellipse that's brought him there.

ASSEZ VU

At Café Vanille I buy a pastry topped
with the sun and its still reflection,
two sugar-glazed apricots
poised to meet on the horizon.

One checkmark on this tour of town.
Goodbye frayed map, oh neat
plotting of events. I round
the corner onto the side street,

and learn what the city thinks
about my sentimental travels:
our park redressed in chain-link,
the grass gone under gravel.

While I sit to think if this is chance
or chastening, a terrier, broken free,
sloshes coffee from the cup in my hand,
draws a muddy streak across my knee.

SLEEPING SONG

When my alarm buzzed him to work before dawn,
he turned and weighed his leg on both of mine,
pressing against my stomach with his palm.

By the time I woke again, the median line
jumped and wavered in his eyes as it swept
to a home I'd never seen. He closed the blind

and slept all afternoon and while he slept,
he dreamt that he was a genius and dead,
the rest of us lost in that dark night, left

with books of numerical tables, with stale bread
and the sound of flies. All the time he was lying
there dreaming, he also thought of me, the bed

I woke alone in striped with light, crying
out at my fingers' work. It was nearly done
as he started to dream what was real, sighing

up into life, thinking he would go out soon
for a drink, that he would see me turn, a sentence
half out of my mouth, look, and he'd be gone.

IV

LUCKY

The staggered line of teeth pushing back toward
their original chaos, the bracelets of condensation
left on tables, cameos of chipped pottery, clothes
turning into moth lace or a lace of broken threads.
It's easy to think everything is a disaster, but then,
look how lucky I've been in this body. And you,
though your scars are worse for lack of stitching,
though you swear it's since you lost that lucky
lighter that your luck's gone sour, act like those
too-healthy doctors who don't believe in conditions
like Lyme disease or fibromyalgia. As far as they
know, the aches come from a dozen causes or none.
And this two-lane highway so accident ready
the sign we just passed nicknamed it Blood Alley—
it's clearly exaggeration. Even those twinges
in the ankle, the ligament's impudent tricks,
aren't enough to address to God or medicine.

DANCE OF DEATH

What would they want? Surely not
this sappy ballad, this slide-show parade
of flowers on display. It was a Friday
afternoon in April, at the memorial
for students who had died, and one of mine,
suicide in early spring, was on the screen.
Then came the headshot of a student I forgot
between crocus-in-snow and peony/rainbow.

Both men young, but one was withdrawn,
the other a know-it-all. As a voice tolled
out the proper nouns, elsewhere in town
the kids were already ramping up their party
with weekend death, contemporary sketches
of Hans Holbein: a skeleton holding
the beer bong, a skeleton popping the tire
of his parents' old car on a curb, a skeleton
puking his missing guts into the tulip bed.

I've always said I wasn't afraid of death,
but still they want you to get the transplant
or the breathing device or whatever else
will keep you alive and whoever loves
you happy. The dance goes on, the best
and worst of us, all will be replaced,
and if you believe everything they say,
this very minute a sucker is born.

Poor purple-faced rube, little rooster.
Give him the suction hose, attach some
censors to his big head. Let him beg,
bribe, whatever. He'll end up like them,

unshaven and unhappy, or else like us, tearless
at a perfunctory ceremony that ends
with *alma mater*, song of the bountiful
mother, which trips through the same
yearning notes no matter where it plays.

LIKENESS

Nine windows, arched and Romanesque,
muster along one wall. They recall
a lover who stretched canvases into antique shapes,
arranged like altar pieces. These he covered
with a muddle of flesh colors, marked with his
apostle's name. His *Magnificat* became
the dream of a little kicker who swelled
my stomach at night and seemed to enlarge
the morning, as clear as the cold unstained
glass of the reading room windows. The catalog
I flip through has been in someone's studio.
A carmine thumbprint in the margin
has not escaped the librarian, who noted
the damage last June among the dates due.
Some works in this book I've seen in life:
ploughed rows ridged with snow, paint matted
with straw or hair, the imagined ascension
over wood-grained stairs or through an opening
in the line of winter trees. Between the library's
marble-papered columns stand faux-bois
metal shelves, empty and filmed with dust.
Overhead the scrollwork moldings, rosettes
sculpted in plaster, alternate with aerated
acoustic tiles, humming grids of fluorescent light.

COMPACT MIRROR

So kind through jostlings and rough use
with gum wrappers and pennies at the bottom
of my bag. I accept the modest compass
of your reflections, the circle that holds the mouth
and part of the chin or just one eye and temple.
Thank you for this partitioning, for vision
that doesn't force wholeness, unwilling
to look at the entire face, which defies our best
attempts to interpret it. A movie director
says the close-up shot always works
because we can't get enough of looking
at human faces. They never come forward
to our desire, entirely readable—as Warhol
knew, with his hours of audition tapes.
The subject left alone, film rolling,
for too long to pose would eventually tire
or get bored, relax, and appear to forget
the camera. Then I get nervous, watching
for her tics or jitters. So much easier
to look at his Marilyns. Seeing her portraits
I expect, if I can look hard enough, to find
some correspondence, her face emerging
as emblem of what she wanted and why.
Of course this will never happen. Open
my eyes while kissing and I get your point:
what we see does not disclose, no matter
how we want it to. Knowing love makes
most sense when it's too close to look at,
we're no less captive to the face we hold
between our hands. How kind, the moment's
relief of compulsion, your refusal even to return

vanity's eye. Thank you, at last, for the hinge
that closes you in on yourself, the complaisance
with which you go back into the purse.

SIGHT GAGS

All I could see in the play
microscope—not puddle
water or spit I squeezed
from an eye-dropper
onto the slide and covered
with a glass flake—was eye-
lashes. In the movies,
a tiptoeing walk signifies
hilarious stealth. A magnifying
glass distorts the detective's
searching eye. But why
does the outsized robot baby
on the news make laymen
squirm when he rolls his
eye-cameras at the scientist
while the diapered chimp
droops his lids and inspires
belly-laughs? What does
intelligence mean beyond
the ability to see and to seem?
At a party once, a veterinary
ophthalmologist extolled
the beauty of the animal
fundus, blue, black or red,
with veins radiating from
the optic disc, tie-dyed moon
in the microscope lens.
Galileo called the instrument
occhiolino, little eye, but he's
better known for shrinking
the cosmos eye-size. He built

a telescope out of organ pipe,
molded glass, and polishing
abrasives. This we know
from his shopping list,
which also reminded him
to buy soap, combs, and sugar.

REASONS FOR LIVING HAPPILY

The plaque on the wall points to a crisis,
but to me she looks composed as she draws
time out, sitting to swing her legs off
the side of the diving platform. In the gallery
space, a tower of bare lumber holds up high
the screen on which she is projected
in her yellow two-piece suit. Standing
next to you in my winter coat and scarf,
looking up at the woman's back where
my hand wants to rest, I wonder if this
is how you feel when you see me half-dressed,
turned to consider the contents of a drawer.
Presumably the installation has something
to say about doubt, but I'm happy just
for the view of the lake beyond the board
and the looped minutes of her leisure.

MEDALLION

Face framed by an umbrella dyed saffron
like his robes or a rainbow-fringed umbrella
or an umbrella made of peacock feathers
or, here, the Dalai Lama's face in full color,
resin-coated and framed by the gold-plate rim
of a coin made to commemorate some occasion
inscribed on the reverse in letters I can't read.

Her face and hair yellow in an aqua background,
her Polish and French surnames written above
her head with the word *Radioactivity* below—
whether it was stolen outright or misplaced
during a move, the university's stained-glass
three-quarter profile of Marie Curie ended up
at auction, where it was recognized by an alum
who used to haunt the library's Polish collection.

During the war, Curie sent small vials of radon
to turn their destructive energy on the necrotic
tissue in the soldiers' wounds. An early scholar
of cancer cures, she may have been curious
to hear His Holiness address the Society
for Neuroscience on finding an ethic for innovation.
Some reviled him as a guru. Some studied his brain
and found it changed by meditation. His face
on a pocket medal. Hers leaded in the window.

THE GALLOW BALL (1950)

repaired in 2001

Smartass conservator, I sense
some misgivings about memory
in your cut-and-paste job. Funny
I just met someone who lost

words like *incongruous, syllabus,*
though he remembers *Stefanie* at least
some of the time. As you'd have it,
these mid-century materials

(oil and newspaper on canvas)
comprehend *Bush* and *Chirac,*
an account of their energy summit
glazed in the painting's abstract eyes.

A scar follows the curve of an ear
through my new friend's hair.
Under its ridged turning the recent
past may slip, like the *susurrus*

released from the shell stashed
in pieces in my desk. For some time
he forgot how laughing is supposed
to follow a joke. How will we learn

the rule again? To where will those
you obscured, strike-breaking *Auriol,*
Truman the Independence boy,
retreat? And then dancing master,

so sure in your intervention, tell me
what to make of this title, which should I
look for first, the turn or the execution?

SPIRITUAL EXERCISES

after Ignatius

Under a bleary moon, the beetles
move to avoid my footsteps. An aimless
obscenity throbs and fades from a passing car.

We must make ourselves indifferent
to all created things: the sun-faded
curtain, wool sweater scratching my neck.

In a café window, the dazzling
side of a semi trailer erases everything
for a second before the street reappears,

parked cars reflected in the glass opposite.
The exercises require silence and someone
to serve as guide. *Ask for sorrow, affliction.*

Instead I listen for carpenter bees
beneath the porch's perpetual light.
Some night, work will come to an end

for men and women and for animals.
I fill my freezer with bones and trimmings.
Our intentions, he says, *should be simple.*

A bowl of pink and orange roses. Apartment
blocks, snow in the mountains. Untranslatable
phrase meaning something like all things
that are good. The almost-wilting roses.

NOTES

"Reform, Missouri": *Give their hearts to the winds of the abyss* is a loose translation of a phrase from René Char's *Leaves of Hypnos*. *No incident but sorrow* is from Oscar Wilde's *De Profundis*.

"Blind King": The italicized phrases are from *King Lear* except for *Before I got my eyes put out*, which is the first line of an Emily Dickinson poem.

"The General": *The one landscape that we, the subconscious ones, hope will blow away* refers to Auden's "In Praise of Limestone" and *I didn't want him on that train, need him on that train* echoes Jack Nicholson in *A Few Good Men*.

"There's something quieter than sleep": The title is a line from a Dickinson poem.

"Permanent Collection": The drain cover with image of Laocoon is a sculpture by Chris Morrey, one of a pair titled "Drain Snakes."

"*The Gallow Ball* (1950)": Painting by Grace Hartigan.

"Reasons for Living Happily": Francis Ponge said that one should be able to give all poems this title.

"Spiritual Exercises": The italicized phrases are from Ignatius Loyola's *Spiritual Exercises*.

Praise for Previous Winners of the Vassar Miller Prize in Poetry

Club Icarus, by Matt W. Miller

"A down-to-earth intelligence and an acute alertness to the gritty movement of language are what you'll treasure most in Matt Miller's *Club Icarus*. You just might pass this book on to a friend or relative who needs it, or even better yet, purchase their own copy."

—**Major Jackson**, author of *Holding Company* and judge

"In Matt Miller's deeply satisfying collection, there is a visceral longing that cannot be ignored, a surrender to the body's fate but also a warring against it. There is the tenacious blood-grief for the lost father but also the deeply abiding yet fearful love of the new father. At the heart of these wonderful poems is a naked wrestling with all those forces that both wither life and give it bloom, those that rob us and those that save us."

—**Andre Dubus III**, author of *House of Sand and Fog*

"In a stunning array throughout Matt W. Miller's remarkable *Club Icarus* are instances of the kind of poetic alchemy that coaxes beauty and a rather severe grace out of the most obdurate materials and unlikely contexts. Here is a poet in whose artful hands language has become an instrument that enables us to know the world again and, simultaneously, as if for the first time."

—**B. H. Fairchild**, winner of the National Book Critics Circle Award for Poetry

"In *Club Icarus* the universal themes of birth and death, love and loss—are woven together with a luminous, transcendent brush. This book is a sly and beautiful performance."

—**Marilyn Chin**, author of *Rhapsody in Plain Yellow*

Death of a Ventriloquist, by Gibson Fay-LeBlanc

"Whether he's overhearing a conversation in a tavern or the music stuck in his head, Fay-LeBlanc uses his ventriloquist to raise important questions about how we perform ourselves through language.

The tension that permeates his poetry—what is seen and unseen, said and eavesdropped, true and trickery—culminates in a debut that rings out long after Fay-LeBlanc's lips stop moving."

—*Publishers Weekly* starred review

"What drives the poems in this wonderfully animated debut volume and prompts the reader's pleasure in them is the patent honesty of the poet's voice. In the 'ventriloquist' series itself, Fay-LeBlanc creates a remarkable refracted self-portrait, bristling with moments of unabashed illumination."

—**Eamon Grennan**, author of *Out of Sight*

"In the words of visual artist Paul Klee, 'art doesn't reproduce what we can see, it makes it visible.' The turf of these poems is a 'vision country' in which our narrator/ventriloquist makes visible (and audible) the world to which he restlessly attends."

—**Lisa Russ Spaar**, author of *Satin Cash* and judge

"Gibson Fay-LeBlanc is a new poet with an old voice. The ventriloquist here throws his own voice while sitting on his own knee, speaking for, but not to, himself, making magic in (and of) plain sight."

—**Brenda Shaughnessy** author of *Human Dark with Sugar*

Circles Where the Head Should Be, **by Caki Wilkinson**
"Playful and soulful, buoyant and mordant, snazzy and savvy—Caki Wilkinson's poems pull out all the stops, and revel in making the old mother tongue sound like a bright young thing. Lend her your ears and you'll hear American lyric moxie in all its abounding gusto and lapidary glory, making itself new all over again."

—**David Barber**, Poetry Editor, *The Atlantic*

"*Circles Where the Head Should Be* has its own distinctive voice, a lively intelligence, insatiable curiosity, and a decided command of form. These qualities play off one another in ways that instruct and delight. An irresistible book."

—**J. D. McClatchy**, author of *Mercury Dressing: Poems*, judge

"Caki Wilkinson's marvelous and marvelously titled *Circles Where the Head Should Be* contains poetry as dexterously written as any today. And beneath its intricate surface pleasures lie a fierce intelligence and a relentless imagination constantly discovering connections where none had been seen before. This is a stunning debut."

—**John Koethe**, author of *Ninety-fifth Street*, winner of the Lenore Marshall Prize

"Like Frost, Wilkinson believes in poem as performance, showing off her verve and virtuosity. She is the 'Lady on a Unicycle,' negotiating her difficult vehicle through the pedestrian crowd with 'the easy lean achieved/ by holding on to nothing'—a joy to witness."

—**A. E. Stallings**, author of *Archaic Smile* and *Hapax*

Stray Home, by Amy M. Clark:

Two poems from *Stray Home* were selected by Garrison Keillor, host of *A Prairie Home Companion* and of *The Writer's Almanac*, to be included in *The Writer's Almanac*, broadcast May 28 and 29, 2010.

"*Stray Home* is a great read. The poetic form found in its pages never feels forced or full of clichés. Whether you are a fan of formal verse or just like to 'dabble,' *Stray Home* is a collection to pick up."

—*Good Reads*

Ohio Violence, by Alison Stine:

"In the mind, Ohio and violence may not be words immediately paired—pastoral cornfields, football fields, and deer versus the blood and splintered bone of a fight or a death. Yet *Ohio Violence* achieves that balance of the smooth and vivid simmer of images and the losses that mount in Alison Stine's collection."

—*Mid-American Review*

"Shot through with a keen resolve, *Ohio Violence* is an arresting, despairing book that alternately stuns and seduces."—*Rain Taxi*

"One comes away from *Ohio Violence* newly impressed with the contingency and instability of the hazardous universe that is our home; and impressed, as well, with the ability of these stark, memorable poems to distill that universe into language and to make of it a sad and haunting song."

—**Troy Jollimore**, *Galatea Resurrects #13*

Mister Martini, by Richard Carr:

"This is a truly original book. There's nothing extra: sharp and clear and astonishing. Viva!"

—**Naomi Shihab Nye**, author of *Fuel*, judge

The Next Settlement, by Michael Robins:

"Michael Robins' prismatic poems open windows, then close them, so we're always getting glimpses of light that suggest a larger world. With never a syllable to spare, these poems are beautiful and haunting. I know of nothing like them."

—**James Tate**, winner of the 1992 Pulitzer Prize for Poetry

"*The Next Settlement* is a finely honed, resonant collection of poems, sharp and vivid in language, uncompromising in judgment. The voice in this book is unsparing, often distressed, and involved in a world which is intrusive, violent, and deeply deceitful, where honesty and compassion are sought for in vain, and refuges for the mind are rare."

—**Anne Winters**, author of *The Key to the City*, judge

re-entry, by Michael White:

"Michael White's third volume does what all good poetry does: it presents the sun-drenched quotidiana of our lives, and lifts it all into the sacred space of poetry and memory. He delights us with his naming, but he also makes us pause, long enough at least to take very careful stock of what we have. He makes us want to hold on to it, even as it trembles in the ether and dissolves."

—**Paul Mariani**, author of *Deaths and Transfigurations*, judge

"Here is a book that explores the interplay between interior and exterior landscapes with such generous and beautifully crafted detail that readers will feel they are no longer reading these poems but living them."

—**Kathryn Stripling Byer**, Poet Laureate
of North Carolina 2005–2009

"In Michael White's latest opus, figure after figure emerge from chaotic ground of memory, such verdant upswellings an urgent music pressured up from deep wells before subsiding—high waterlines left in our wake to mark the turbulence of love's intractable flood."

—**Timothy Liu**, author of *For Dust Thou Art*

The Black Beach, by J. T. Barbarese:

"*The Black Beach* constantly delights with its questing, surprising, and not-easily-satisfied imagination. But simultaneously it creates an exacting and exhilarating vision of 'God, the undoer that does.' The speaker who, in one poem, stands in the moment 'love / what is not,' is the same one who, in another poem, imagines 'the black beach of heaven where all desire / is merged, twinned, recovered, braided, and set ablaze.' "

—**Andrew Hudgins**, author of *Ecstatic in the Poison*, judge

"A dark brilliance shines in these honed, memorable poems of the human predicament: that of a sentient particle with a mind for the infinite. 'Looking for meaning/ the way radio waves sought Marconi,' Barbarese's restless imagination searches through the stations of the daily to the 'very end of the dial/ the static that never signs off,' and turns back to receive what we have, the 'lonely surprised heart/ shaken . . .'"

—**Eleanor Wilner**, author of *The Girl with Bees in Her Hair*

"Barbarese has an uncanny ability to size up the urban scene, then hallow and harrow it. Putting his daughter on the local train for the city, he conjures up those who rode in the boxcars to the ovens. And, leaning over 'winged rot . . . glued . . . to shat-on grass' in a nearby park, he can think 'how beautiful,/ the hard frost had cemented/ what had lived to what never did.' He wins me over in poem after poem."

—**Maxine Kumin**, author of *The Long Marriage*

Losing and Finding, by Karen Fiser:

"There are so many delights in this book, interpenetrated by so many losses. . . . She keeps her eye unflinchingly on 'the rough loving arms of this world,' even as she is buffeted about by it."

—**Lynne McMahon**, judge

"From the searing heart of pain and patience come the transporting poems of Karen Fiser. Trust them. Treasure them. These poems are resounding, important, and deeply humane."

—**Naomi Shihab Nye**, author of *Fuel*

Bene-Dictions, by Rush Rankin:

"*Bene-Dictions* is a canny, unnerving book. Its cool manners seem to hold compassion at bay; but its irony is a cleansing discipline which allows it to conjure complex lusts, hurts, and injustices without self-pity and, apparently, without delusion. These poems describe a world in which 'Tenderness is an accident of character/ or energy, or just a side-effect/ of having failed at what you wanted,' but in which the reader, to read the effect of rain on paper, 'opens the book/ in a storm, as though to find the world itself in tears.'"

—**Rosanna Warren**, author of *Ghost in a Red Hat* and judge

"If the long hours in offices of the mind elect for us meaningfulness, they must always eventually find the human heart. Then Rankin's vivid and surprising poems map that movement where as Rilke insists, what is sublime is mundane, and everything that falls must somehow in shadow/act, rise."

—**Norman Dubie**, author of *The Mercy Seat: Collected and New Poems 1967–2001*

The Self as Constellation, by Jeanine Hathaway:

"This is a collection to be read in sequence because the continuity is powerful and persuasive. If we are attentive readers, we end like the nuns in the storm cellar 'not knowing whether we've been struck by lightning or by love.'"

—**Madeline DeFrees**, author of *Blue Dusk: New and Selected Poems, 1951–2001* and judge

The Perseids, by Karen Holmberg:

"It is a rare pleasure to encounter these days a young poet so thoroughly at home in the natural world, so deeply attuned to its mysteries, that reading her book we enter, in turn, that 'Spherical Mirror,' the elemental mind which, as *The Perseids* reminds us, forms 'the core of human bliss.'"

—**Sherod Santos**, author of *The Intricated Soul:*
New and Selected Poems and judge

A Protocol for Touch, by Constance Merritt:

"Merritt's prosodic range is prodigious—she moves in poetic forms as naturally as a body moves in its skin, even as her lines ring with the cadenced authority of a gifted and schooled ear. Here, in her words, the iambic ground bass is in its vital questioning mode: 'The heart's insistent undersong: how live? // how live? How live?' this poetry serves no lesser necessity than to ask that."

—**Eleanor Wilner**, author of *The Girl*
with Bees in Her Hair and judge

Moving & St rage, by Kathy Fagan:

"Kathy Fagan's long awaited second collection keeps revealing new strengths, new powers. Its words are of unsparing rigor; its intelligence and vision continually spring forward in changed ways. These are poems both revealing and resistant: deeply felt, deeply communicative, yet avoiding any easy lyricism. Again and again the reader pauses, astonished by some fresh turn of language, of insight, of terrain. *Moving & St rage* offers extraordinary pleasures, clarities, and depth."

—**Jane Hirshfield**, author of *Come, Thief*

"From the first emblems of language—the angular letters of A and K—a child steps toward the preservation of consciousness, and, in turn, the paradox of preserving that which is lost. These beautifully crafted poems trace a journey to adulthood and grief with a lyrical mastery that is breathtaking. *What can language do with loss?* Fagan asks. This splendid book is her answer."

—**Linda Bierds**, author of *Flight: New and Selected Poems*

Soul Data, by Mark Svenvold:

"*Soul Data* is rarely compounded—of wit and music, surface elegance and intellectual depth, quirk and quandary. Its sensual intelligence is on high alert, and the sheer unsheerness of its language—all its densities and textures—is a linguiphiliacal delight. Unmistakably American (the poetry's occasions and its cadences alike serve for signature) it has the jinx-meister's humors about it. A fine rhetorical savvy, in a mind inclined to the chillier depths: among poetic gifts these days it's an uncommon conjunction, a gift of mysteries, like the sight (across a night pond's surface) of bright-blue shooting star: one hopes the other humans get to see it."

—**Heather McHugh**, author of *Upgraded to Serious*

American Crawl, by Paul Allen:

"It is absolutely no exaggeration to say that no one is writing like Paul Allen. There is not an ounce of flab in his poems, which are informed by an urgency, a sense of personal commitment, and a passion rarely seen in contemporary poetry. America in the 1990s is not a comfortable world in which to live; and Paul Allen is certainly not the man to entertain us with fanciful invitations to dens of innocence. Though *American Crawl* is a first book, there is nothing jejune about the poems, or about the unique imagination that creates them. The publication of this book is an important contribution to American letters."

—**Richard Tillinghast**, author of *The New Life*

The Sublime, by Jonathan Holden:

"*The Sublime* embodies a poetry that is personal and public, and shows through clear-cut imagery how varied our imagined and actual lives are. Everything seems to be woven into this ambitious collection: love, war, divorce, fear, anger, doubt, grace, beauty, terror, popular culture, nature. This poetry challenges us to remain (or become) whole in an increasingly fragmented world."

—**Yusef Komunyakaa**, winner of the 1994
Pulitzer Prize for Poetry and judge

Delirium, by Barbara Hamby:

"Barbara Hamby is an extraordinary discovery! A poet of compassion and elegance, she is a poet whose debut in *Delirium* promises a rich (and enriching) lifelong project."

—**Cynthia Macdonald**, author of *Living Wills*

Partial Eclipse, **by Tony Sanders:**

"Sanders brings together his own sensibility (quizzical, approaching middle-age, slightly disaffected, bemused, learned but not stuffy) and an alertness to what can be appropriated from history, myth, the daily papers."

—Choice

". . . a distinguished first collection from a poet about whom we will be hearing more."

—Houston Post

"Sanders proceeds through his . . . poems with a pervasive steadiness of diction, . . . a syntactic resonance quite his own yet gratefully beholden to such exacting masters as Stevens and Ashbery. The freshness of the poems is a result of their immersion in life with others, achieving the resolute tonality of a man speaking not so much out or up but on, talking his way to the horizon."

—Richard Howard, author of *Untitled Subjects*, winner of 1970 Pulitzer Prize for Poetry, and judge

CPSIA information can be obtained at www.ICGtesting.com
Printed in the USA
LVOW12s1221260314

378798LV00002B/2/P

9 781574 415544